HANUKKAH

COLOR BY NUMBER

FOR KIDS

This Book
Belongs To:

_____

_____

HANUKKAH

COLOR BY NUMBER

FOR KIDS

This Book
Belongs To:

_____

_____

1 DARK ORANGE   2 LIGHT BLUE   3 DARK BLUE
4 YELLOW   5 LIGHT ORANGE   6 WHITE
7 PURPLE

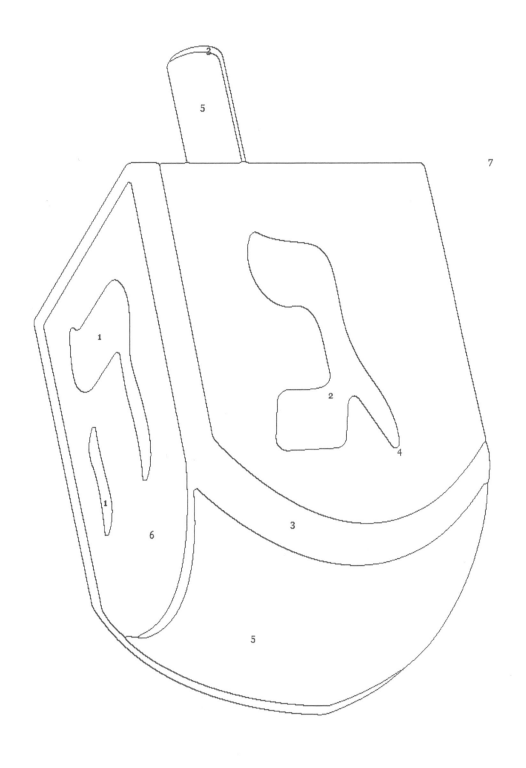

1 RED   2 GREEN   3 LIGHT BROWN   4 DARK ORANGE
5 LIGHT ORANGE   6 SKIN   7 WHITE

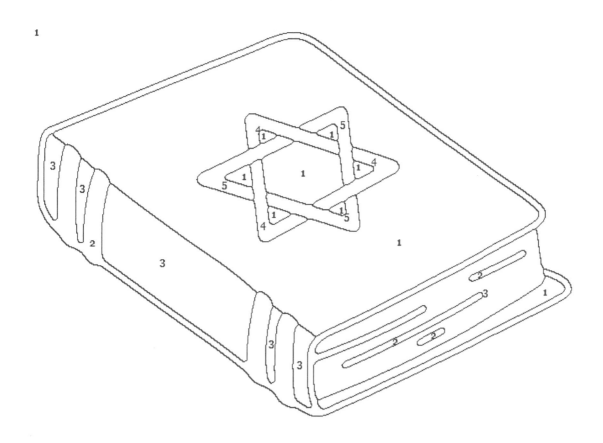

1 WHITE   2 DARK BLUE   3 LIGHT BLUE

4 ORANGE   5 YELLOW

1 LIGHT BLUE　　　2 SKIN　　　3 BLACK　　　4 BROWN

5 RED　　　6 BLUE　　　7 WHITE　　　8 PINK

1 GREEN   **2 SKIN**   **3 PINK**   **4 DARK BROWN**
5 BROWN   **6 LIGHT PINK**   **7 BLACK**   **8 WHITE**

1 RED   2 SKIN   3 DARK BROWN   4 LIGHT BROWN
5 LIGHT PINK   6 WHITE

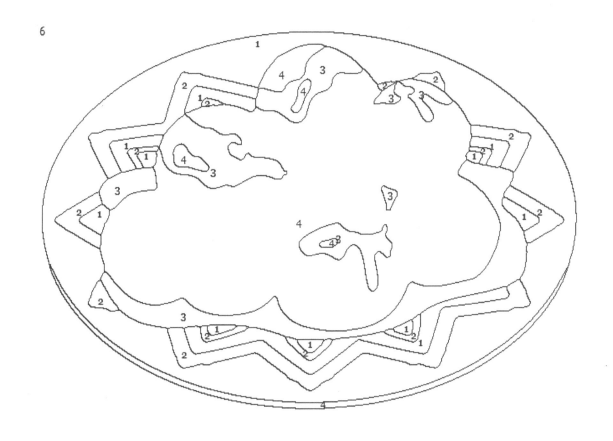

1 LIGHT BLUE   **2 BLUE**   **3 YELLOW**   **4 LIGHT BROWN**
5 LIGHT GRAY   **6 WHITE**

1 YELLOW   2 PINK   3 SKIN   4 PURPLE

5 LIGHT BLUE   6 BLUE   7 WHITE

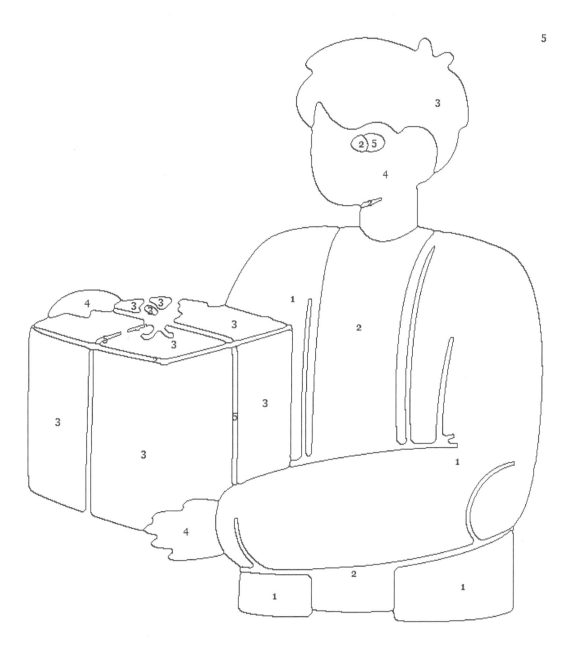

1 YELLOW   **2 BLUE**   **3 PURPLE**

4 BROWN   **5 WHITE**

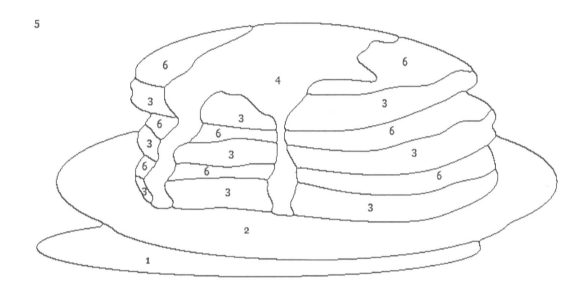

1 BLACK   2 LIGHT BLUE   3 SKIN   4 DARK BROWN
5 WHITE   6 LIGHT BROWN

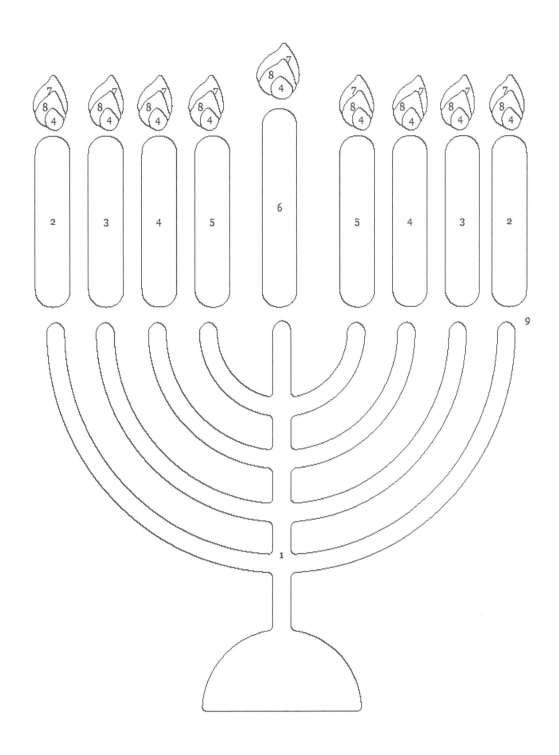

1 SKIN   2 PURPLE   3 DARK ORANGE   4 YELLOW
5 BLUE   6 PINK   7 ORANGE   8 DARK YELLOW
9 WHITE

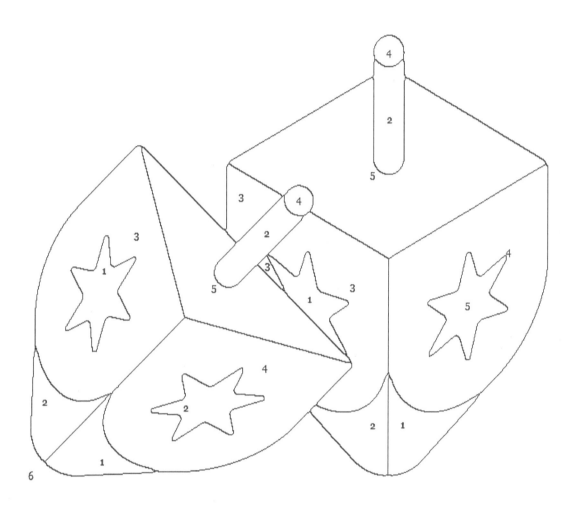

1 BROWN   2 LIGHT BROWN   3 PURPLE
4 BLACK   5 BLUE   6 WHITE

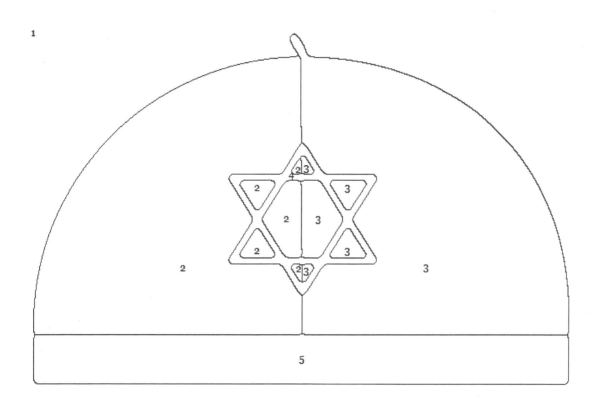

1 WHITE   **2 LIGHT BLUE**   **3 BLUE**
4 BROWN   **5 CHARCOAL**

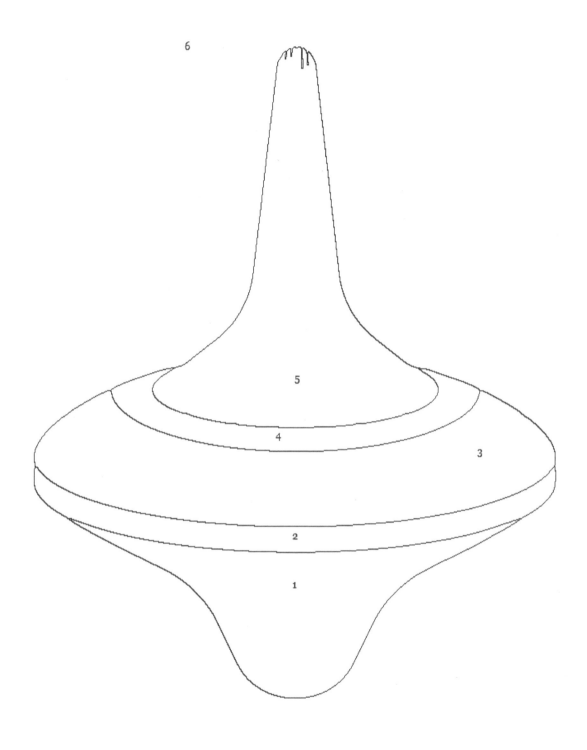

1 PURPLE   2 BROWN   3 ORANGE   4 SKIN
5 BLUE   6 WHITE

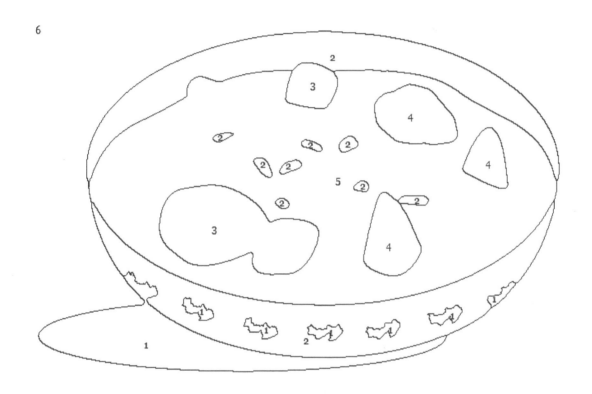

1 BLACK   2 GREEN   3 YELLOW   4 ORANGE
5 BROWN   6 WHITE

1 BLACK   2 GREEN   3 YELLOW   4 ORANGE
6 BROWN   5 WHITE

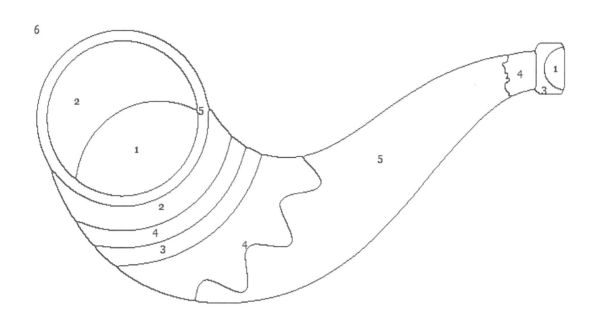

1 BROWN   **2 DARK BLUE**   **3 ORANGE**

4 LIGHT BLUE   **5 LIGHT PURPLE**   **6 WHITE**

1 DARK GREEN **2 BROWN** **3 YELLOW** **4 ORANGE**
5 LIGHT GREEN **6 WHITE** **7 RED**

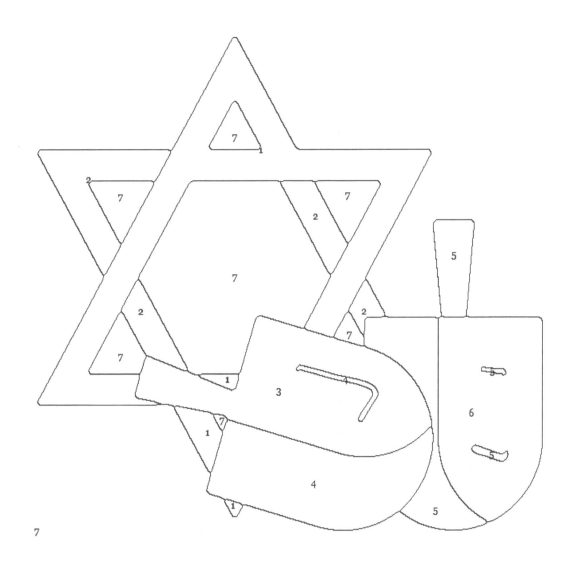

1 DARK YELLOW   **2 LIGHT YELLOW**   **3 LIGHT BLUE**
4 DARK BLUE   **5 DARK PINK**   **6 LIGHT PINK**
7 WHITE

1 BLACK   **2 CHARCOAL**   **3 BROWN**   **4 YELLOW**
5 PINK   **6 GREEN**   **7 DARK ORANGE**   **8 LIGHT ORANGE**
9 WHITE

1. BLACK
2. CHARCOAL
3. BROWN
4. YELLOW
5. PINK
6. GREEN
7. DARK ORANGE
8. LIGHT ORANGE
9. WHITE

1 GREEN   2 BLUE   3 YELLOW
4 ORANGE   5 PURPLE   6 WHITE

1 BROWN   **2 YELLOW**   **3 BLUE**

4 WHITE   **5 ORANGE**

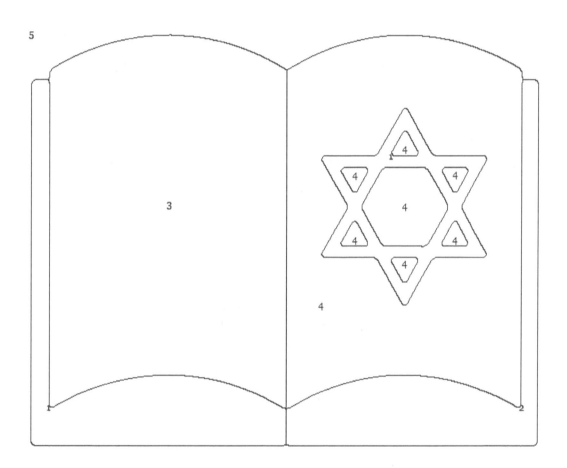

1 DARK BLUE   2 BLUE   3 DARK PINK
4 PINK   5 WHITE

1 SKIN   2 RED   3 DARK BLUE
4 LIGHT BLUE   5 WHITE

1 LIGHT BLUE   2 WHITE   3 SKIN
4 DARK BLUE   5 LIGHT GREEN

1 BROWN   2 SKIN   3 DARK BLUE

4 YELLOW   5 LIGHT BLUE   6 WHITE

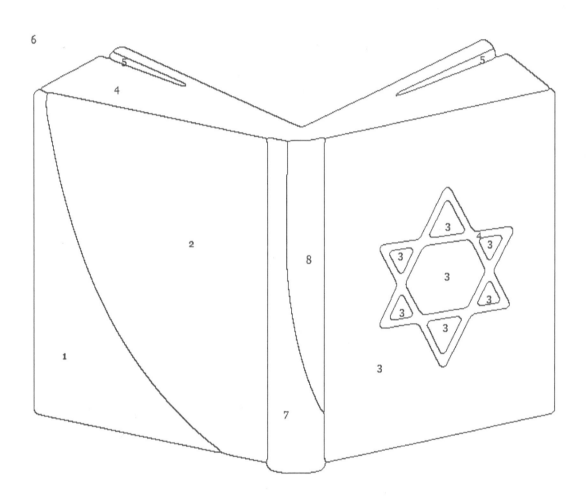

1 LIGHT BLUE   2 LIGHT PURPLE   3 DARK PURPLE
4 SKIN   5 LIGHT BROWN   6 WHITE
7 DARK YELLOW   8 LIGHT YELLOW

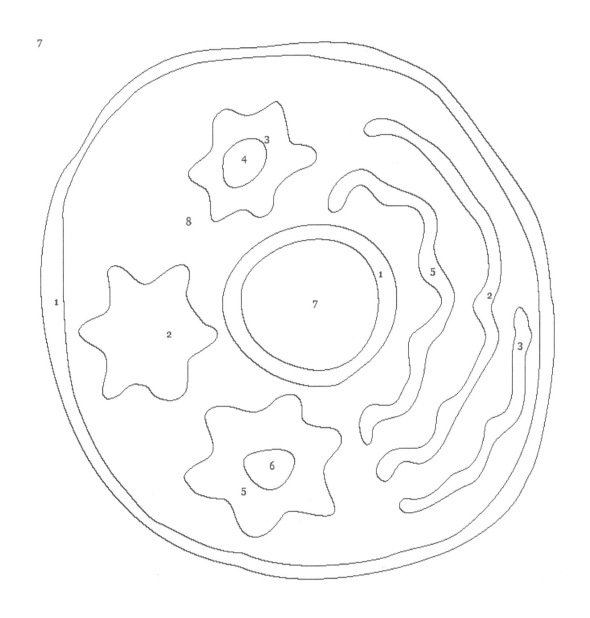

1 LIGHT BROWN   2 LIGHT BLUE   3 LIGHT YELLOW
4 DARK YELLOW   5 LIGHT PURPLE   6 DARK PURPLE
7 WHITE   8 DARK BROWN

1 DARK GRAY   **2 GRAY**   **3 SKIN**   **4 LIGHT PINK**
5 LIGHT BROWN   **6 DARK BROWN**   **7 WHITE**

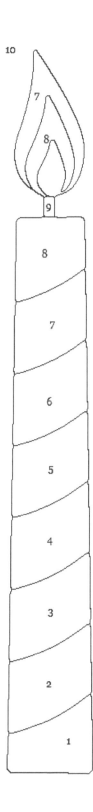

1 DARK BROWN   **2 GRAY**   **3 DARK BLUE**   **4 LIGHT BLUE**
5 DARK PINK   **6 LIGHT PINK**   **7 DARK YELLOW**
8 LIGHT YELLOW   **9 LIGHT BROWN**   **10 WHITE**

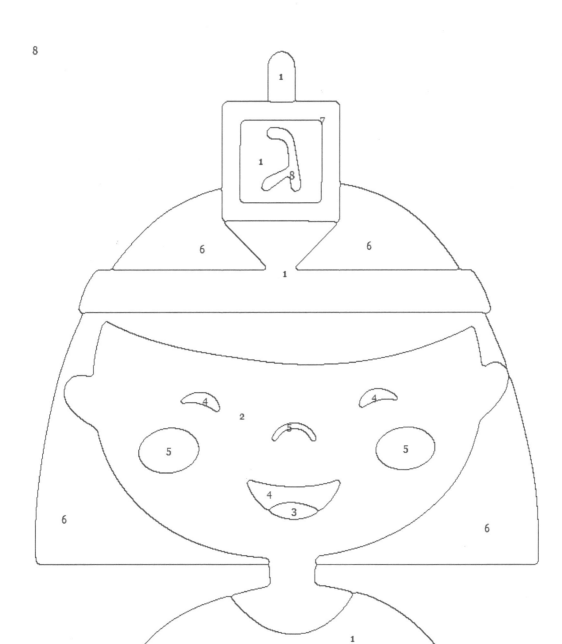

1 LIGHT PINK   2 SKIN   3 RED   4 DARK BROWN

5 LIGHT BROWN   6 YELLOW   7 DARK PURPLE   8 WHITE

1 LIGHT ORANGE   2 SKIN   3 RED   4 DARK BROWN
5 LIGHT BLUE   6 LIGHT BROWN   7 DARK ORANGE
8 WHITE

1 YELLOW   2 GREEN   3 BROWN   4 ORANGE   5 BLACK
6 GRAY   7 LIGHT BROWN   8 DARK PINK   9 LIGHT PINK
10 DARK BLUE   11 LIGHT GREEN   12 LIGHT BLUE   13 WHITE
14 SKIN

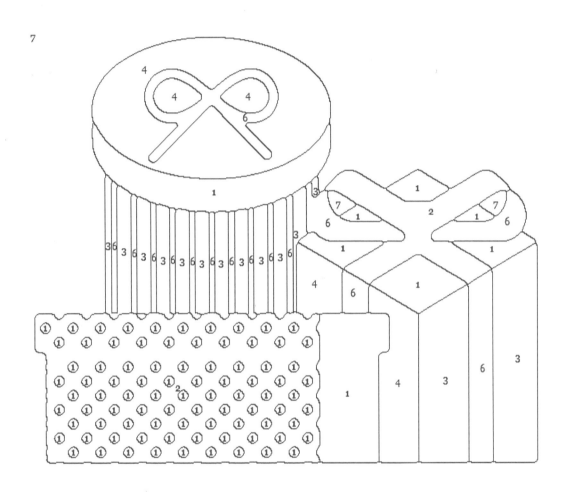

1 DARK BROWN　　**2 LIGHT BROWN**　　**3 LIGHT BLUE**
4 DARK BLUE　　**5 ORANGE**　　**6 YELLOW**　　**7 WHITE**

1 SKIN   **2 YELLOW**   **3 DARK GREEN**   **4 LIGHT GREEN**
5 ORANGE   **6 WHITE**

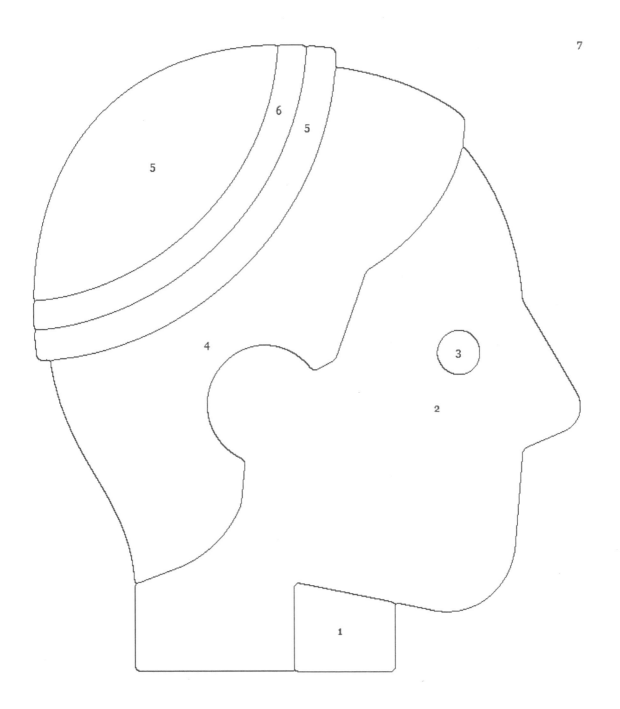

1 ORANGE   2 SKIN   3 BROWN   4 GRAY
5 LIGHT BLUE   6 DARK BLUE   7 WHITE

1 LIGHT BROWN   **2 SKIN**   **3 RED**   **4 BLUE**

5 YELLOW   **6 BROWN**   **7 GREEN**   **8 WHITE**

1 DARK BLUE   2 LIGHT BLUE   3 WHITE
4 ORANGE   5 SKIN

1 LIGHT BLUE   2 LIGHT BLUE   3 PINK
4 LIGHT PINK   5 WHITE

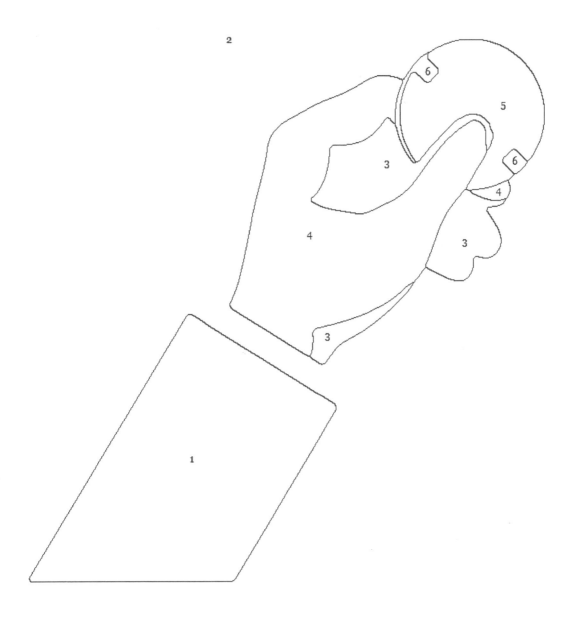

1 LIGHT BLUE   **2 WHITE**   **3 DARK PINK**
4 LIGHT PINK   **5 ORANGE**   **6 BROWN**

**1 DARK BLUE   2 SKIN   3 GRAY   4 WHITE
5 LIGHT GREEN**

Made in United States
Troutdale, OR
12/26/2024

27251557R00046